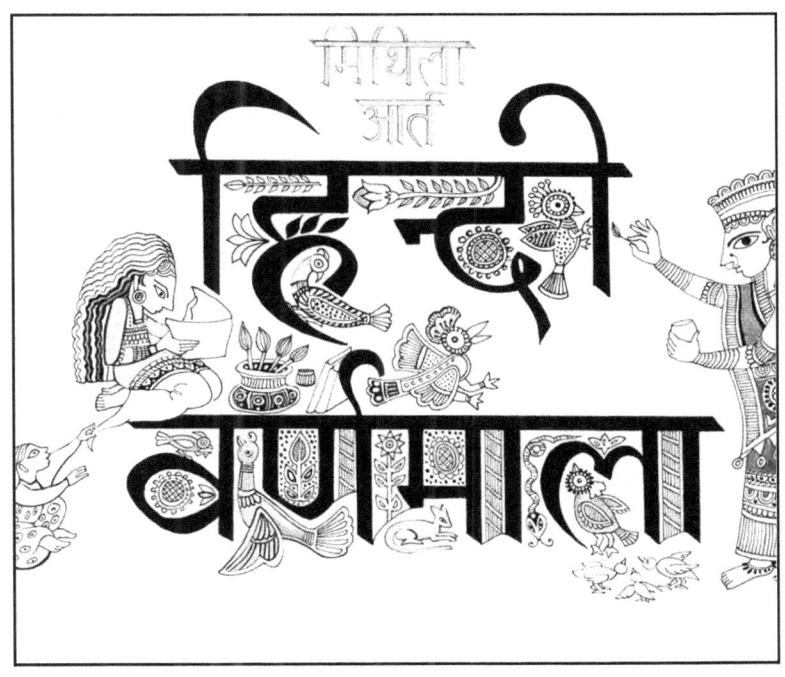

Mithila Reverie

Meditations on the Devanagari Script

by

Martine Le Coz

Ethnic Arts Foundation Press

Mithila Reverie
Published in 2014 by Ethnic Arts Foundation Press.
Title page Hindi text: Mithila Art, Hindi Alphabet

Book Design and Editing: Peter Zirnis
Hindi Alphabet and Translation: Pranjali Sirasao

ISBN 978-0692298-15-2

David Szanton
Ethnic Arts Foundation Press
1417B Spruce Street,
Berkeley, California 94709
szanton@berkeley.edu

FOREWORD

Martine Le Coz is a French novelist and artist residing in Amboise, France. As a student in Tours at the age of twenty she discovered paintings from the Mithila region of Bihar, close by the Nepal border, at an exhibition mounted by Yves Véquaud. Deeply moved by this distinctive ancient wall painting tradition that had recently gone onto paper, and the continuous links from mother to daughter that gave the art its vitality, she never forgot them, nor the women who painted them. Indeed, they inspired her to continue drawing and painting, whatever else she might do.

Later, becoming more familiar with Indian thought, thanks to the eminent scholar André Padoux, her desire grew to meet the women of the central Mithila town of Madhubani and the surrounding villages both to pay homage to them, and to paint their portraits. During several visits there she spent long hours with many of the leading artists who were producing stunning paintings in several related styles, and on a wide and growing array of subjects. Her book that resulted, *Mithila, L'honneur des Femmes*, published by Michalon-L'Harmattan (Paris, 2013), includes the artists' life stories, her portraits of them in a unique integration of their styles and hers, as well as photos of her painting together with them.

While in Madhubani, Martine Le Coz also discovered *The Mithila Art Institute (MAI)*, a free art school founded in 2003 by the Ethnic Arts Foundation when it appeared the painting tradition might soon disappear. She was impressed by the school both because of its demanding curriculum taught by senior artists committed to training a new generation of painters and also because about 95% of the 25 students accepted every year are young women coming from communities as far as 50 kilometers away.

Believing that the work of the Mithila Art Institute is important and that the Mithila art tradition should not die, Martine Le Coz decided to do paintings in the Mithila style on 42 letters of the Indian Devanagari alphabet. Each letter begins a Hindi word that is illustrated by an image that has a deep cultural meaning in the Indian tradition. She then donated the 42 paintings to the Ethnic Arts Foundation to be used to aid the Mithila Art Institute in its mission of training, encouraging and supporting Mithila art and artists.

We hope that this book of her paintings will delight you, perhaps even inspire or help you to learn an Indian language. Proceeds from the sale of the book will go to sustain the Mithila Art Institute and the vitality of the Mithila painting tradition.

David Szanton,
President
Ethnic Arts Foundation

Parmeshwar Jha,
President
Mithila Art Institute

BRIDGING WORLDS
an Introduction

Alphabets that are paintings, paintings that are stories, a book that opens up a window into Indian culture - that is *Mithila Reverie* by Martine Le Coz. Language and script are at the basis of human communication, and art expands several dimensions beyond that, making connections that are universal. The Hindi alphabets made in Mithila style form a symbolic bridge between two different worlds in more ways than one. The compilation reflects a sharing of expression and an intuitive friendship that crosses the boundaries of language and culture.

Mithila painting evolved as a women's ritual art in the region of Bihar in North-east India. The wall based painting tradition was first discovered in the modern period in the early 1930s. Then three decades later, after devastating drought conditions, the rural women were encouraged to use paper as a base for their paintings so these could be sold for income.

Paper transformed the context and purpose of painting. The ephemeral wall and floor drawings that were made with natural colors and twig-brushes as accompaniments to specific celebrations and rites of passage became framed for posterity. The anonymous artist became recognizable as a name and women who privately made their art within a courtyard crossed physical, ideological and conceptual bridges to break away, at least partially, from the boundaries structured by centuries of community tradition. Their art had a greater outreach, and many of the artists became recognized nationally and internationally for their subtle expressions rooted in the legacy of their local history and culture.

Martine Le Coz is articulating integral elements of this women's art and in doing that reveals a sense of oneness with them. Beginning with 'Ahimsa', Mahatma Gandhi's revered and recognized symbol of 'non-violence', moving to simple items like 'Machli' (fish) or mythological and divine characters like 'Varaha' (the divine boar, the third incarnation of lord Vishnu), she deftly introduces the reader not only to the alphabet but to distinct aspects of Indian life and history. Through the book, Martine Le Coz takes the reader through a journey that was perhaps her own experience of the Indian landscape and Madhubani in particular.

Each page comes alive with meticulously drawn lines following the aesthetics and precision of Mithila painting, yet imbued with Martine Le Coz's very own spirit. The lines create patterns and two-dimensional scenes from which emerge the heroines of each piece, the Alphabets. Typical and much loved motifs that inhabit Mithila paintings, including turtles (kachua), owls (ullu), elephants (hathi), flowers (phūl) and other flora and fauna native to the Bihar environment, appear in the book as word-guides to understanding the sounds represented by the alphabets.

Having visited Madhubani in 2012, Martine Le Coz was deeply struck by the strength and boldness of the black, white and red drawings done by women there. She was attracted by the honesty of the expression that seemed elementally connected to their life and environment. Through her interactions with many of the women, she encountered the spirituality and the natural confidence of the speaking lines that they drew. Knowing these women and their art made her want to understand more so she learned to write their names in the Devanagari script. Martine Le Coz says her epiphany came with the realization that as she drew in Amboise, France, women in far away Madhubani were also drawing, concentrating, living and giving their time with similar humility and sharp desire – simultaneously.

In the last forty years Mithila art has come a long way and evolved through contemporary times in the face of varied challenges. With *Mithila Reverie,* Martine Le Coz brings the inherent poetry of the painting style to readers, sharing her love for it. As a writer and a painter, she unites script and drawing, each element supporting the other and merging into one through the visual vocabulary of Mithila art.

Lina Vincent Sunish
Gurgaon, India
September, 2014

The Alphabet

अ

अहिंसा (*ahinsā*) – non–violence

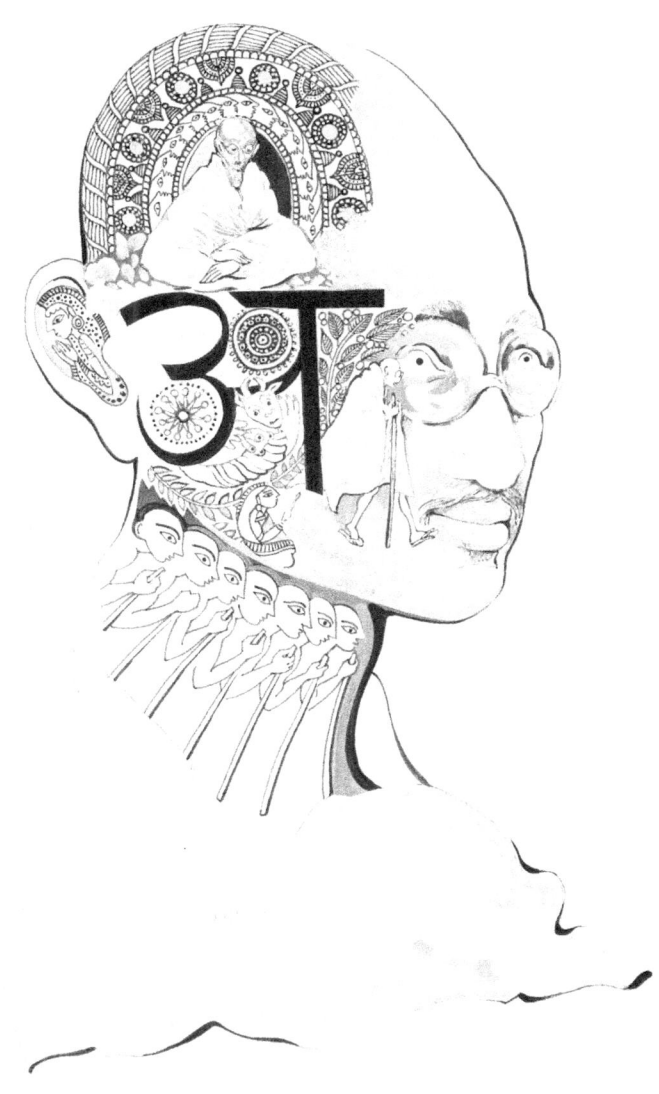

आ

आम (*ām*) - mango

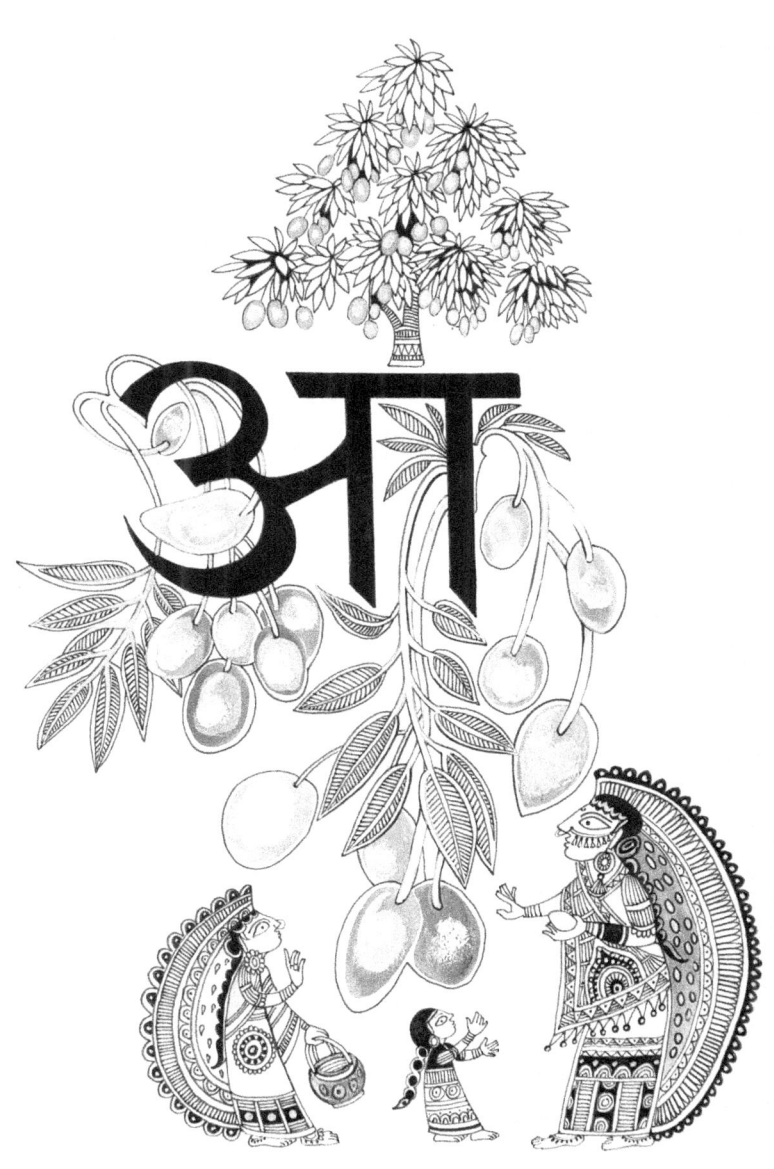

आ

इ

इमली (*imlī*) - tamarind

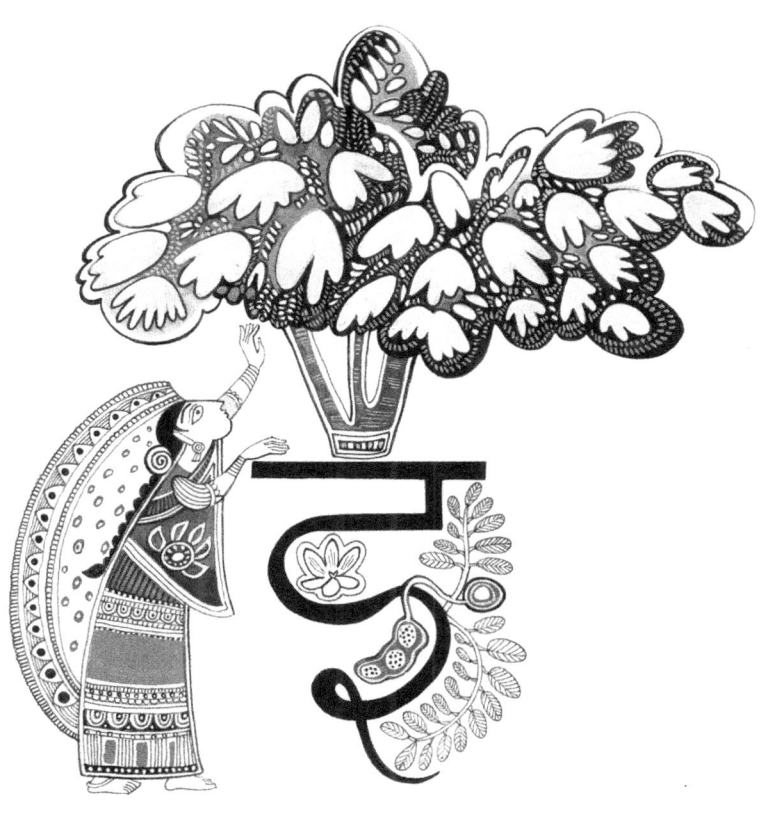

ई

ईख (*īkh*) – sugarcane

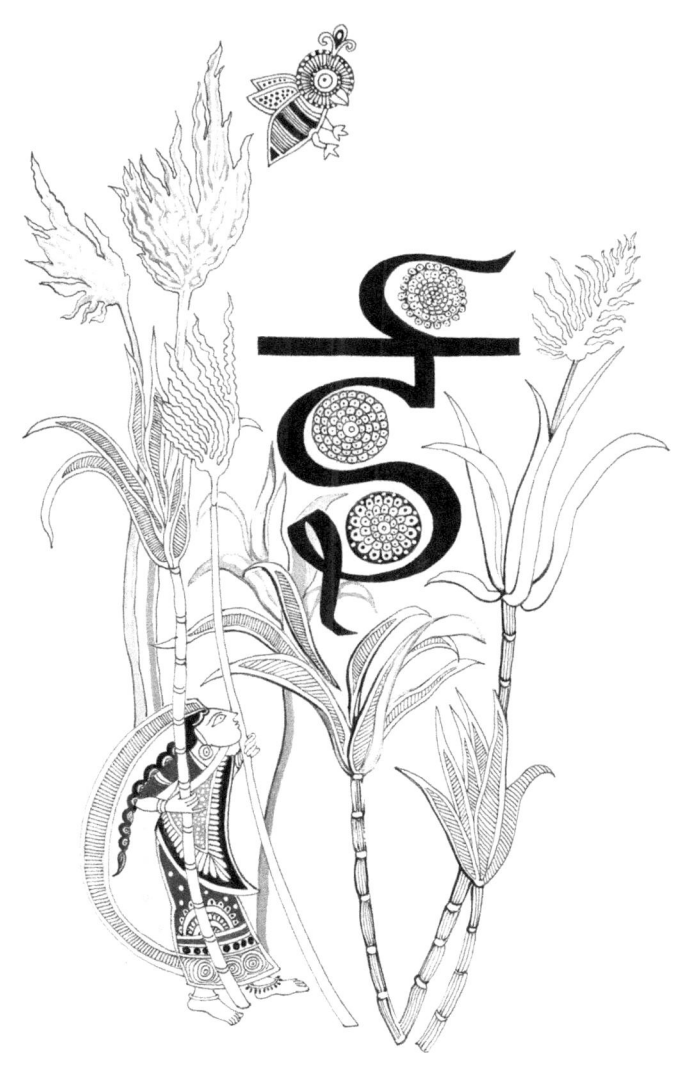

उ

उल्लू (*ullū*) – owl

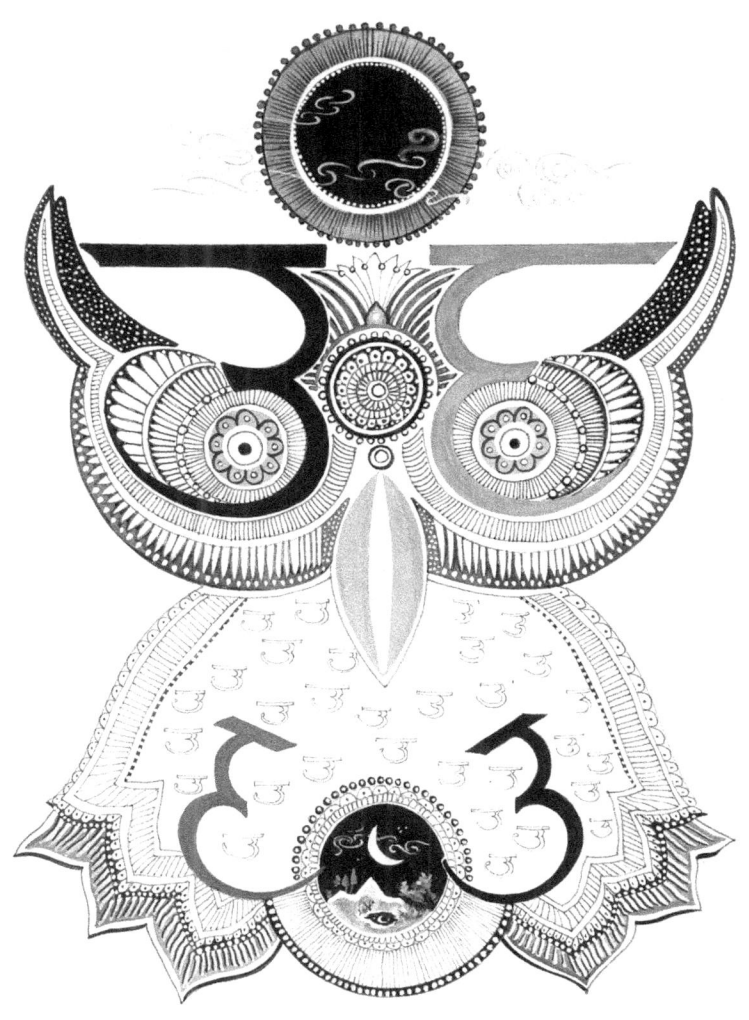

ऊ

ऊँट (*ūnt*) – camel

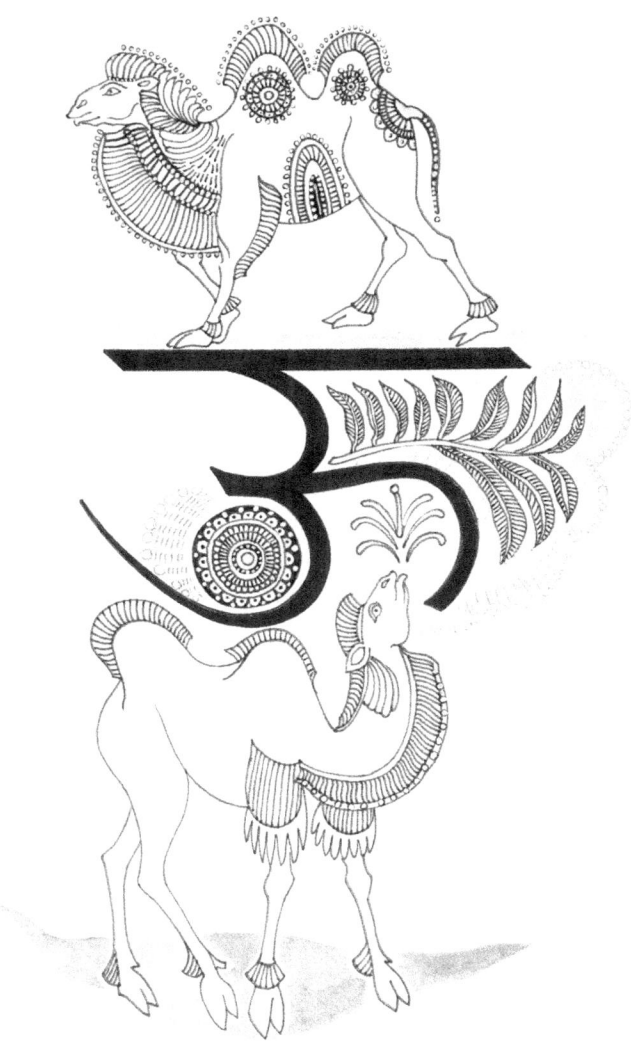

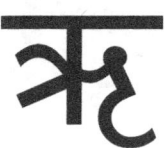

ऋषि (*ṛshi*) – a sage

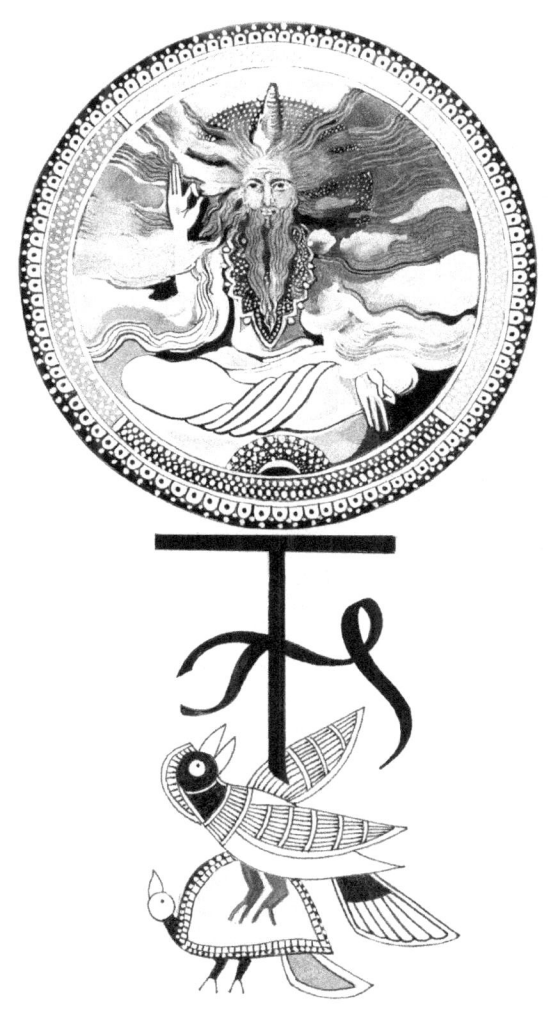

ए

एक *(ek)* – one, unit as in atom

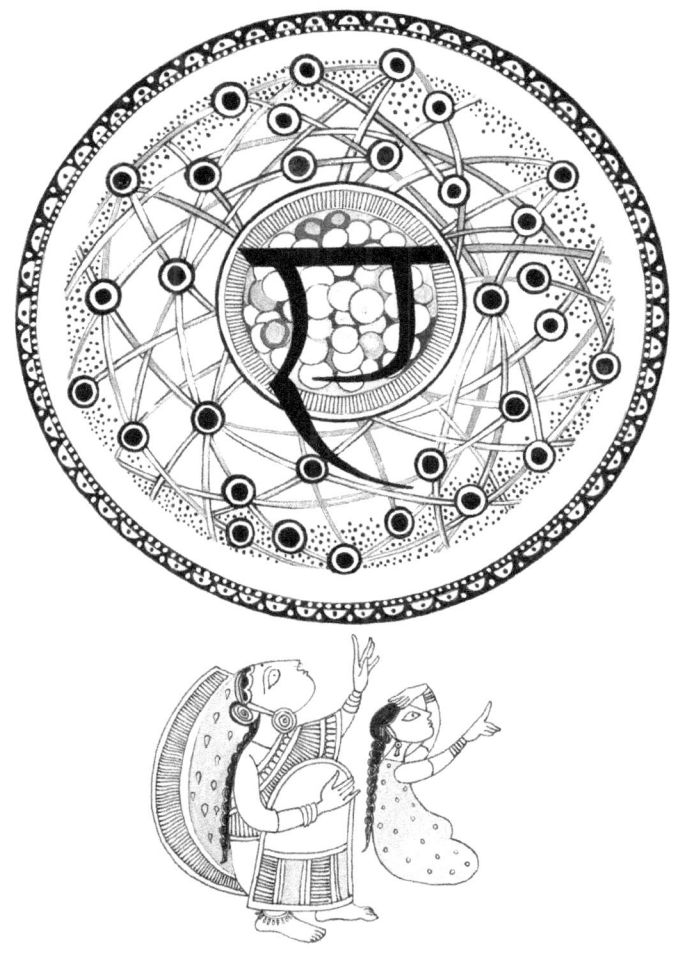

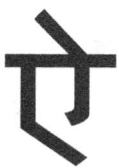

ऐरावत (*airāvat*) – Indra's mythical elephant

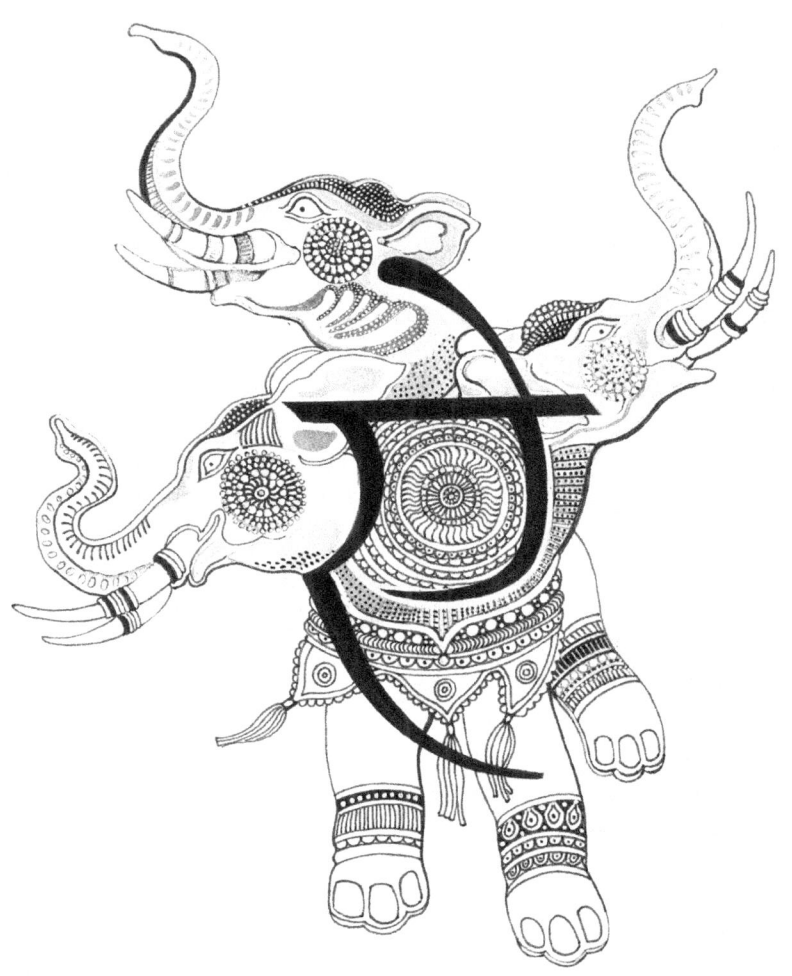

ओ

ओज (*oj*) – energy, vigor

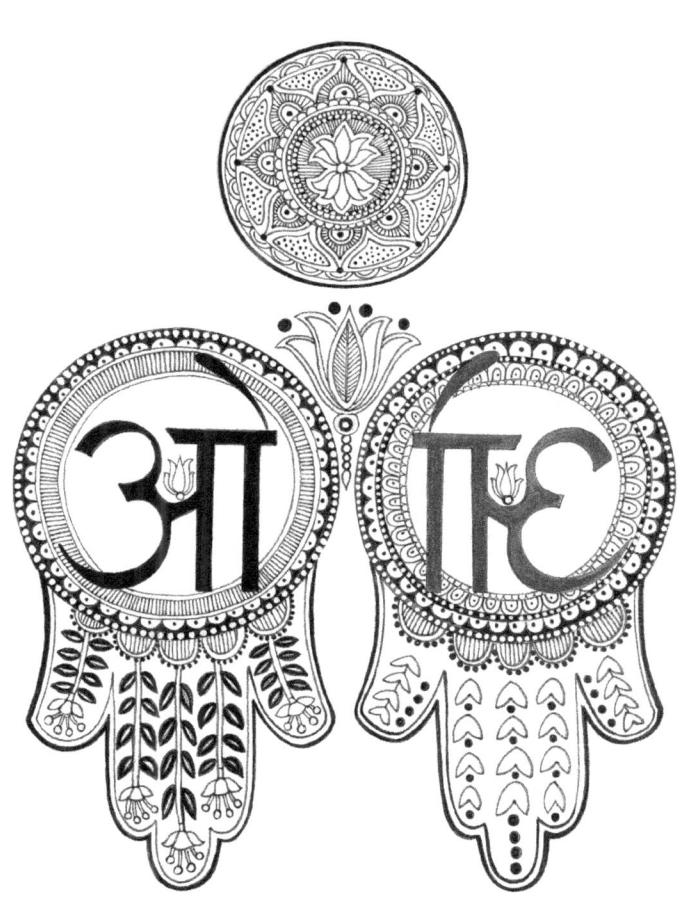

औ

औषधि (*aushadhi*) – medicine

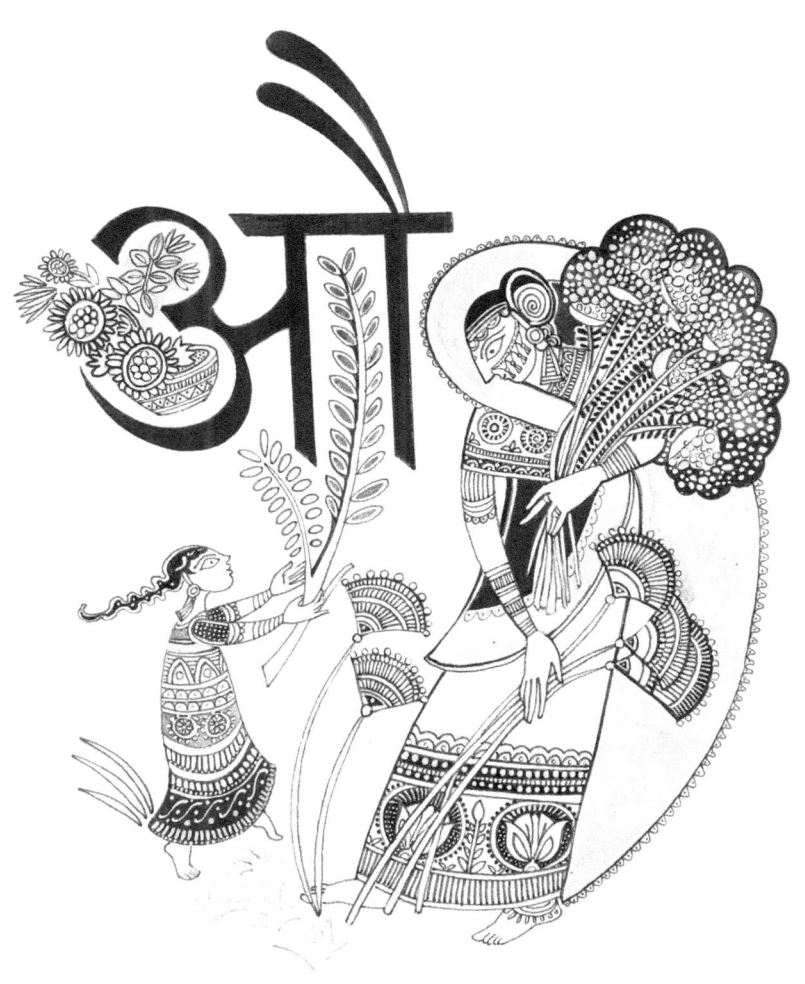

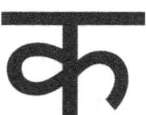

कछुआ (*kachuā*) – tortoise

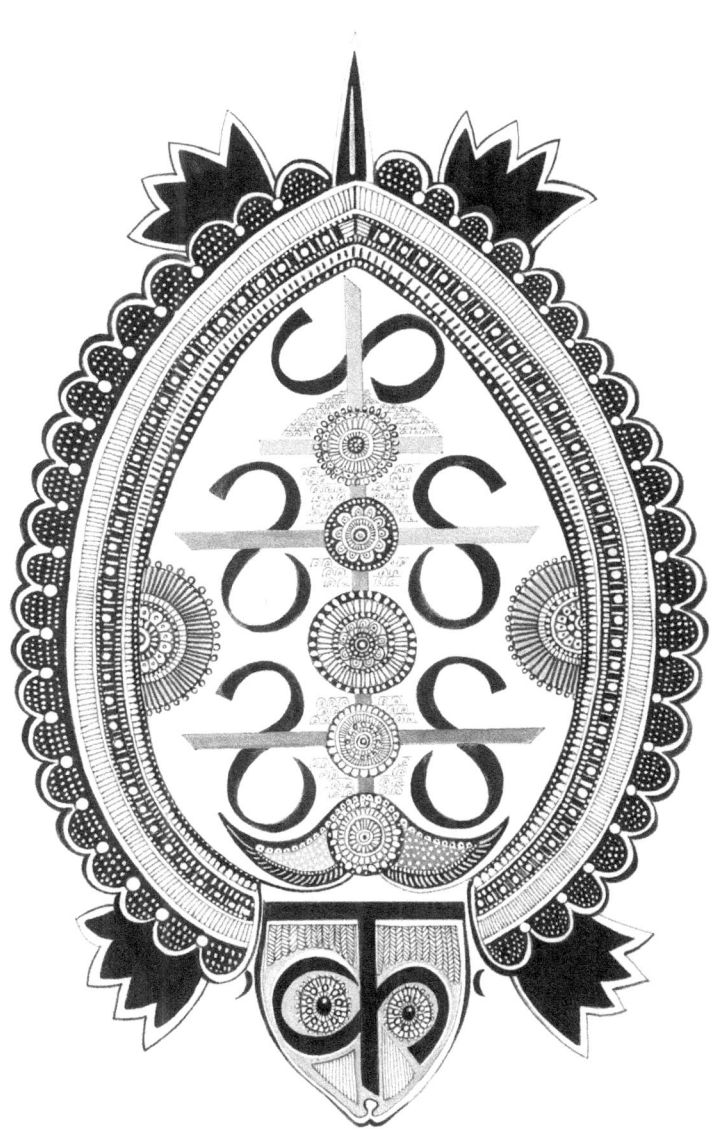

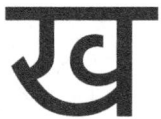

खरगोश (*khargosh*) – rabbit

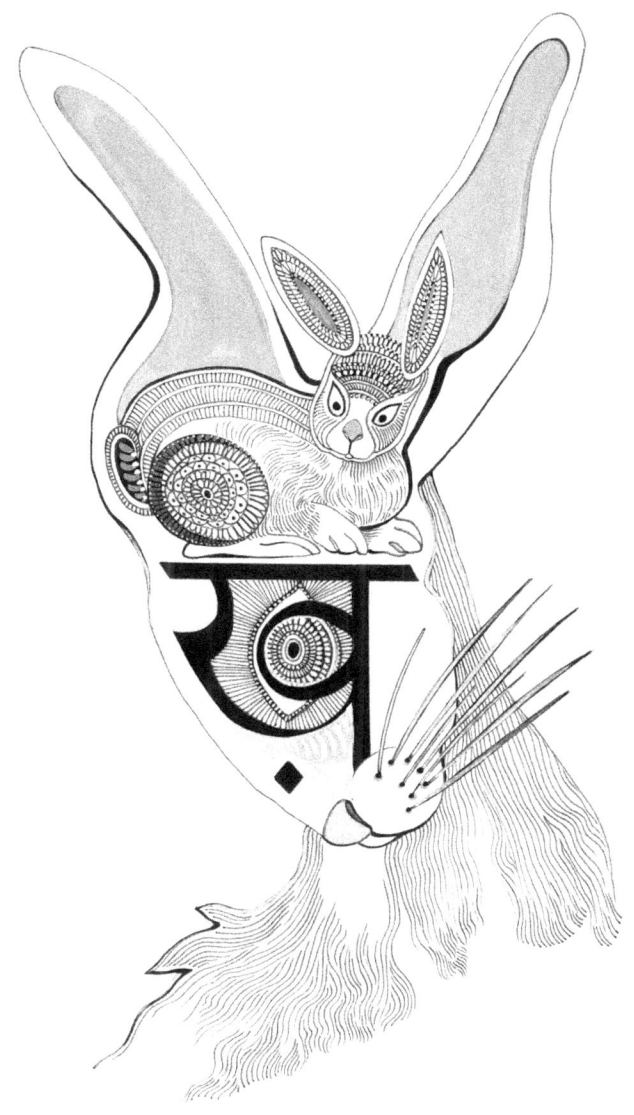

ग

गाय *(gāy)* – cow

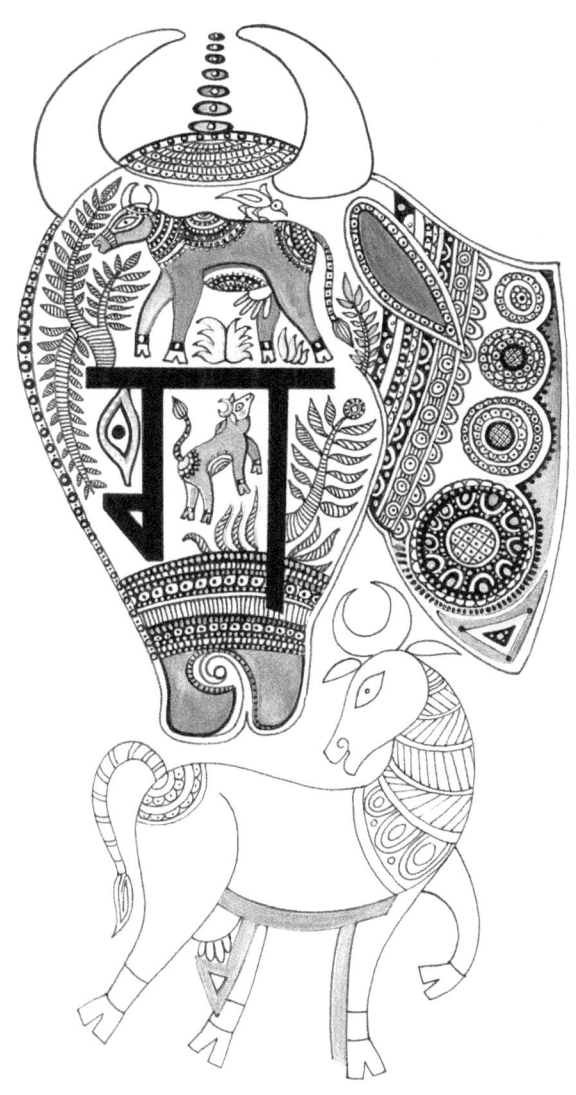

घ

घोंघा (*ghongā*) – snail

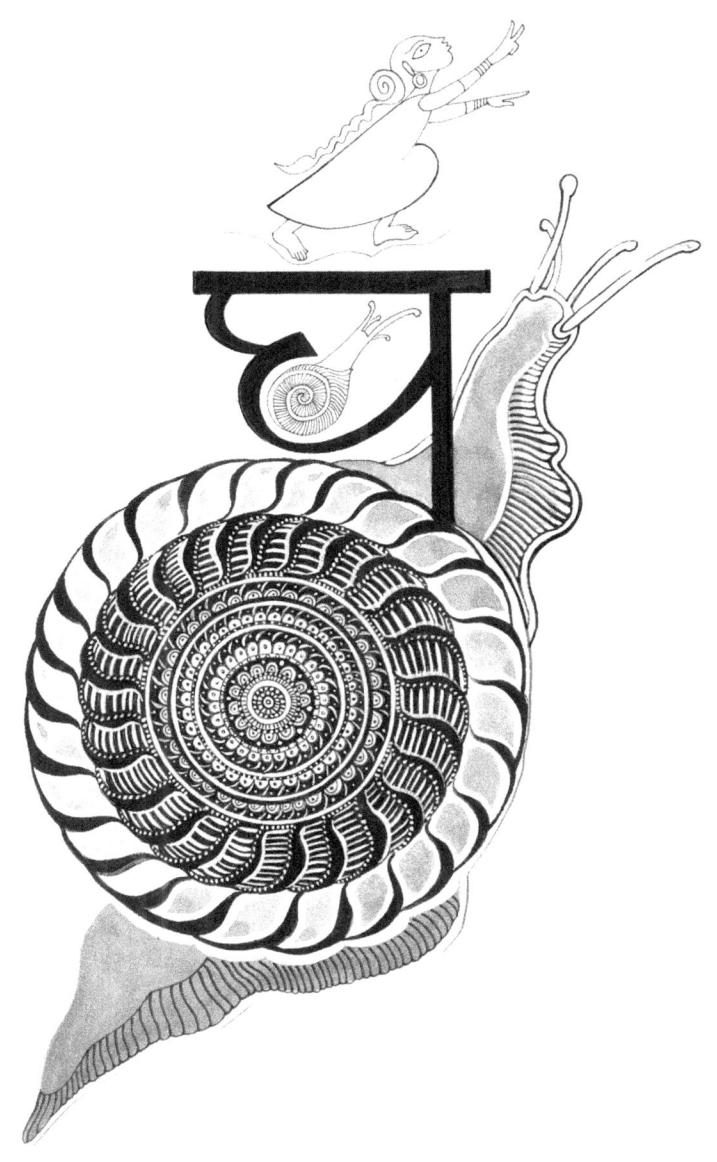

च

चूहा (*chūhā*) – mouse

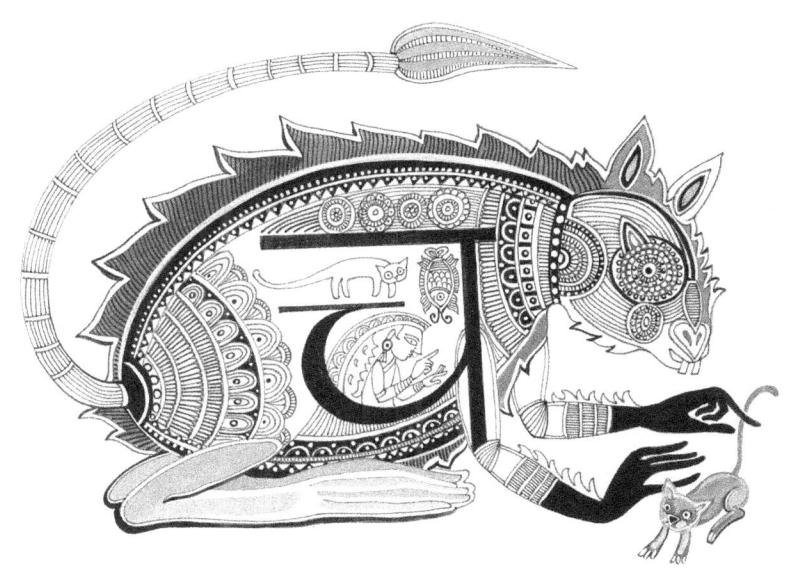

छ

छिपकली (*chipkalī*) – lizard

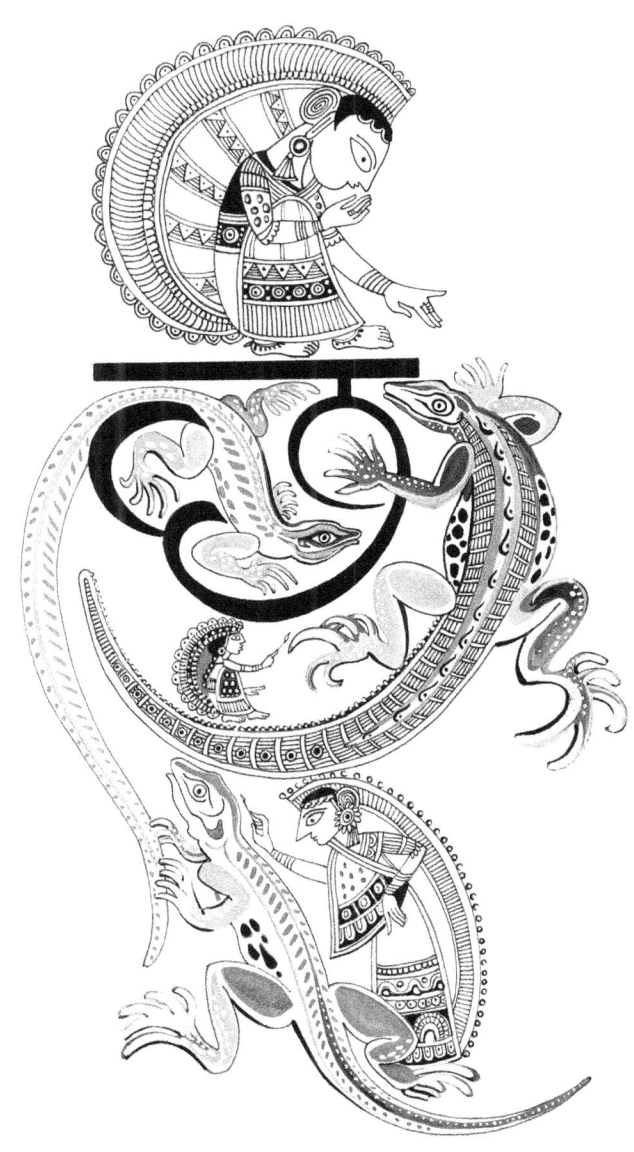

ज

जेलीफ़िश (*jelīfish*) – jellyfish

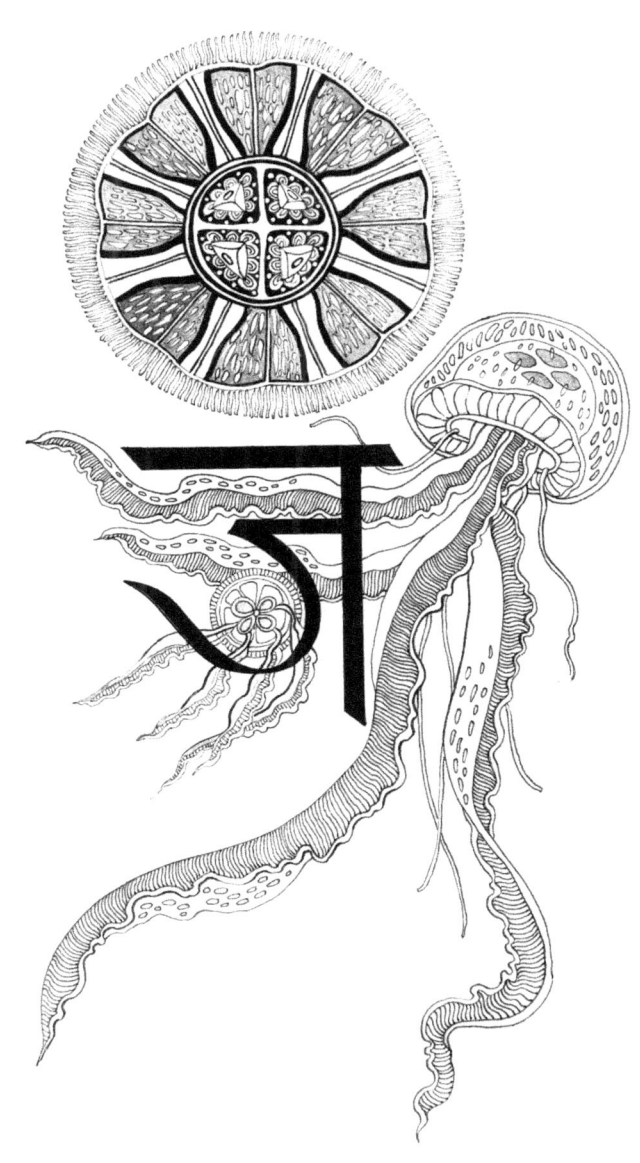

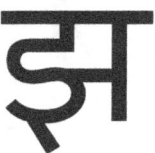

झींगा (*jhīngā*) – prawn or shrimp

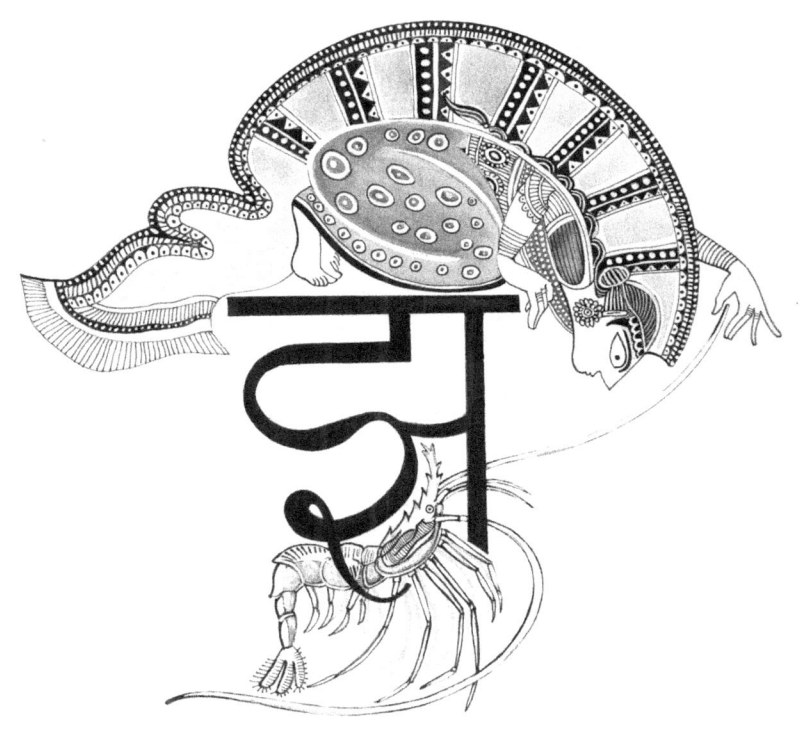

ट

टर्की (*tarkī*) – turkey

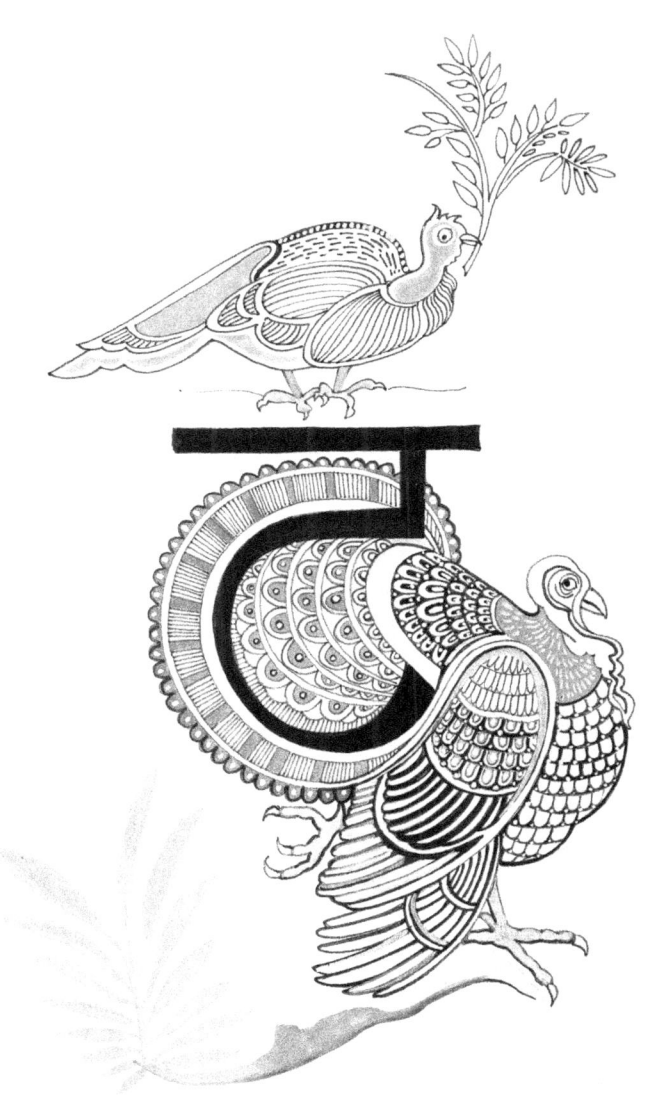

ठ

ठंडाई (*thandāī*) – thandai, a milk based
beverage served during festivals.

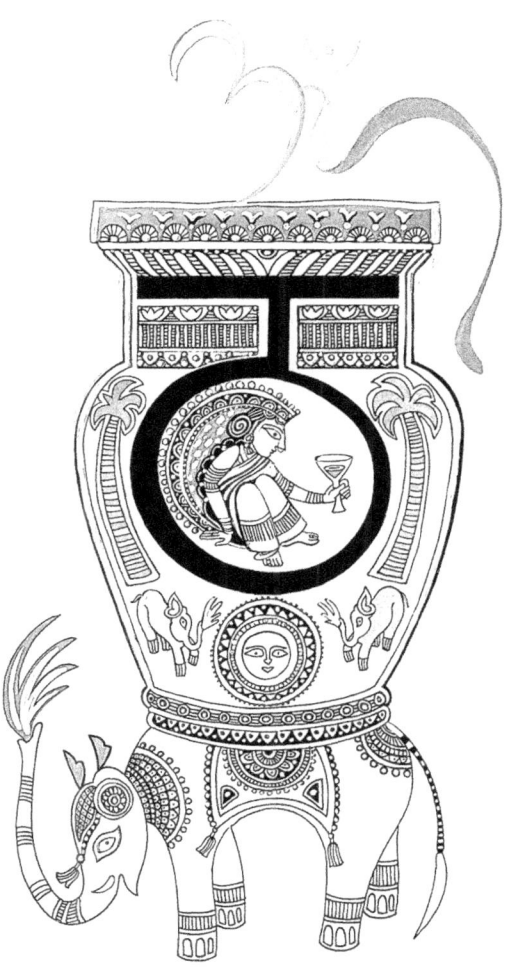

ड

डाली (*dālī*) – branch of a tree

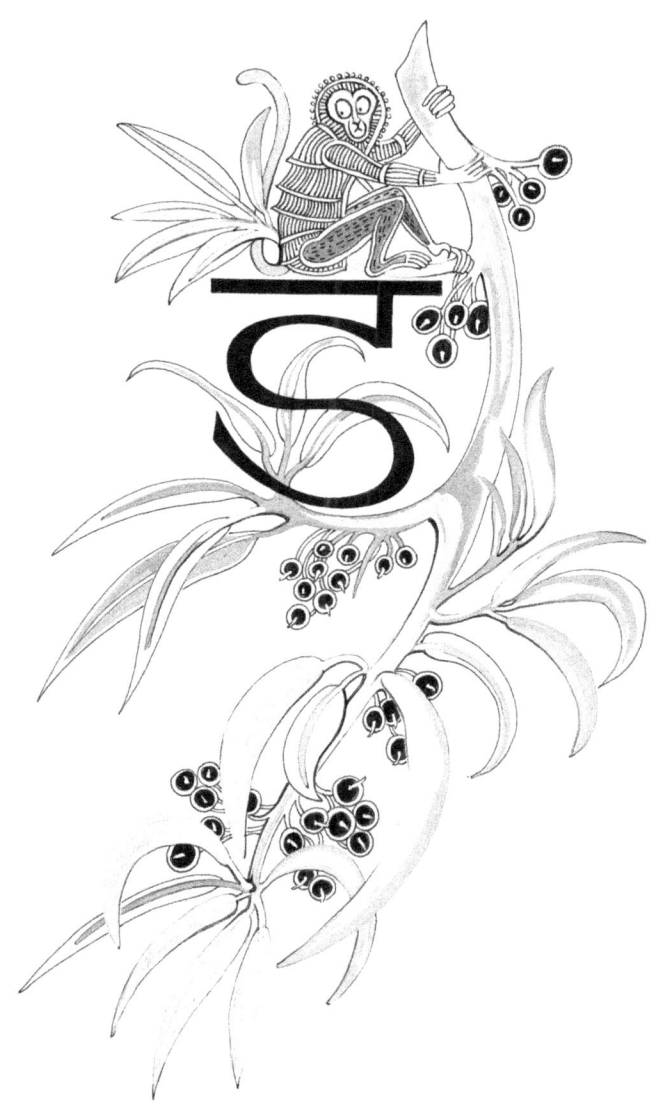

ढ

ढलकना (*dhalaknā*) – to flow. A pregnant
woman crossing her fingers for her water to flow.

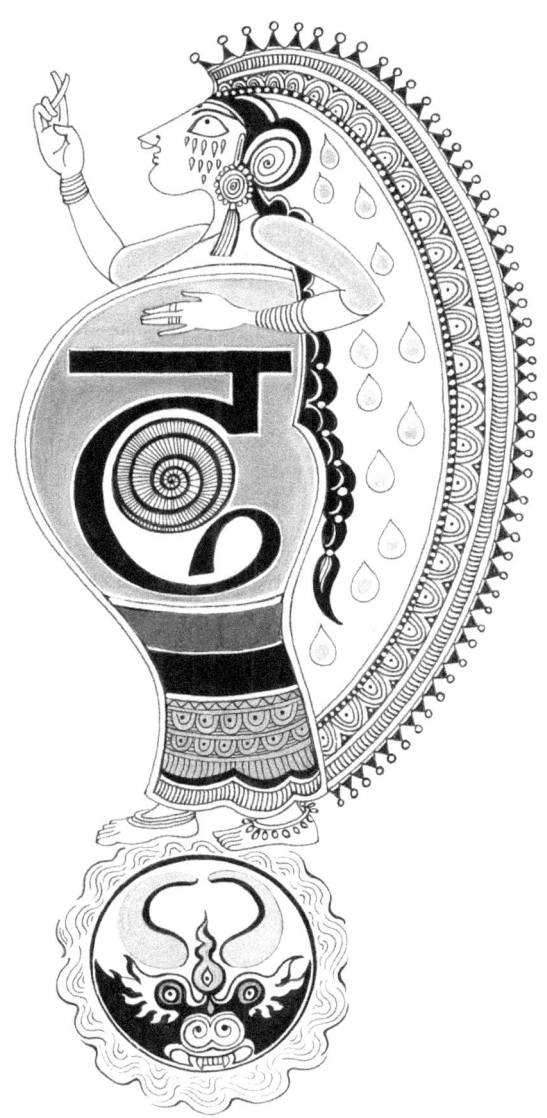

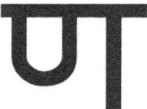

ण *(ṇ)* – second letter of the word Ganesh

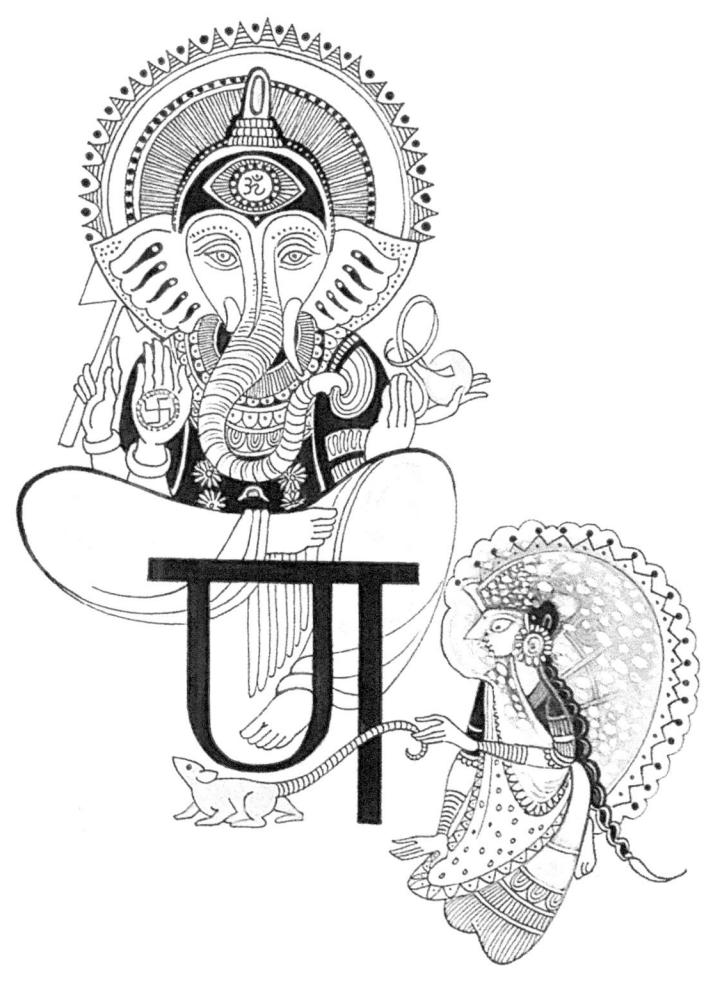

त

तितली (*titlī*) – butterfly

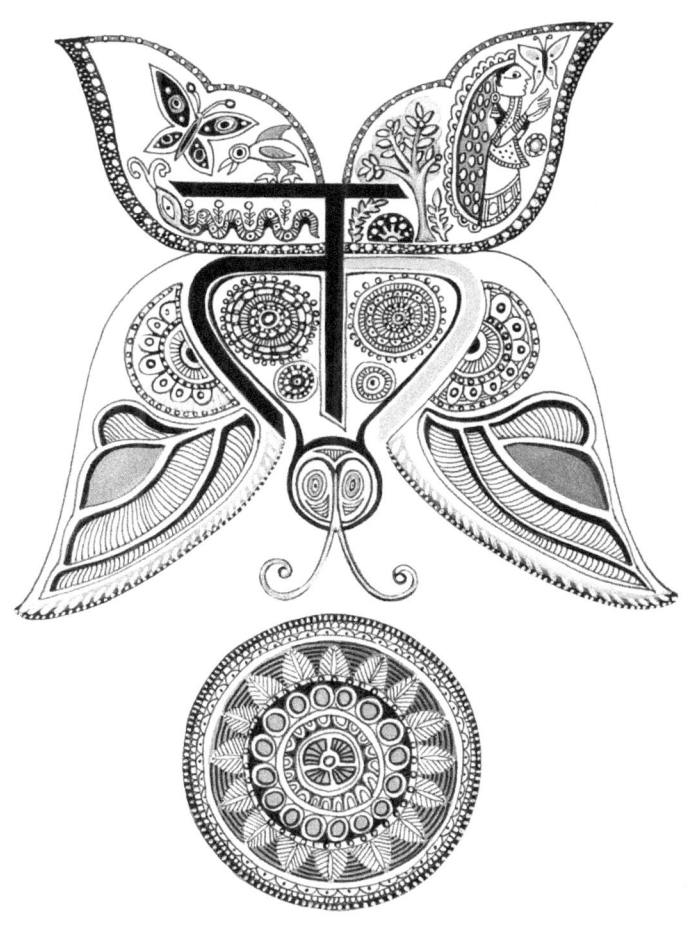

थ

थिरकना (*thiraknā*) – dance move

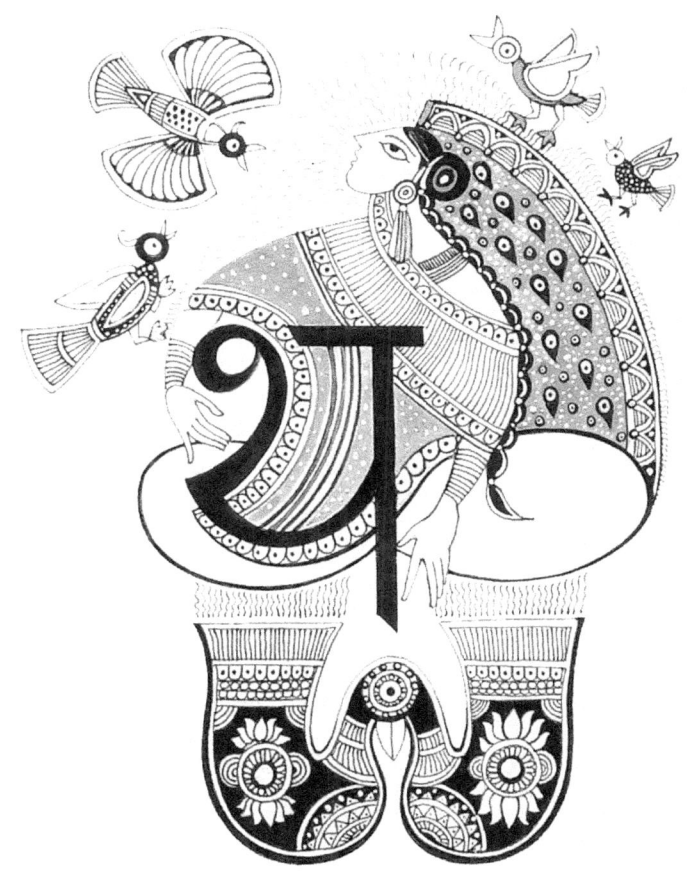

द

दीमक (*dīmak*) – termite

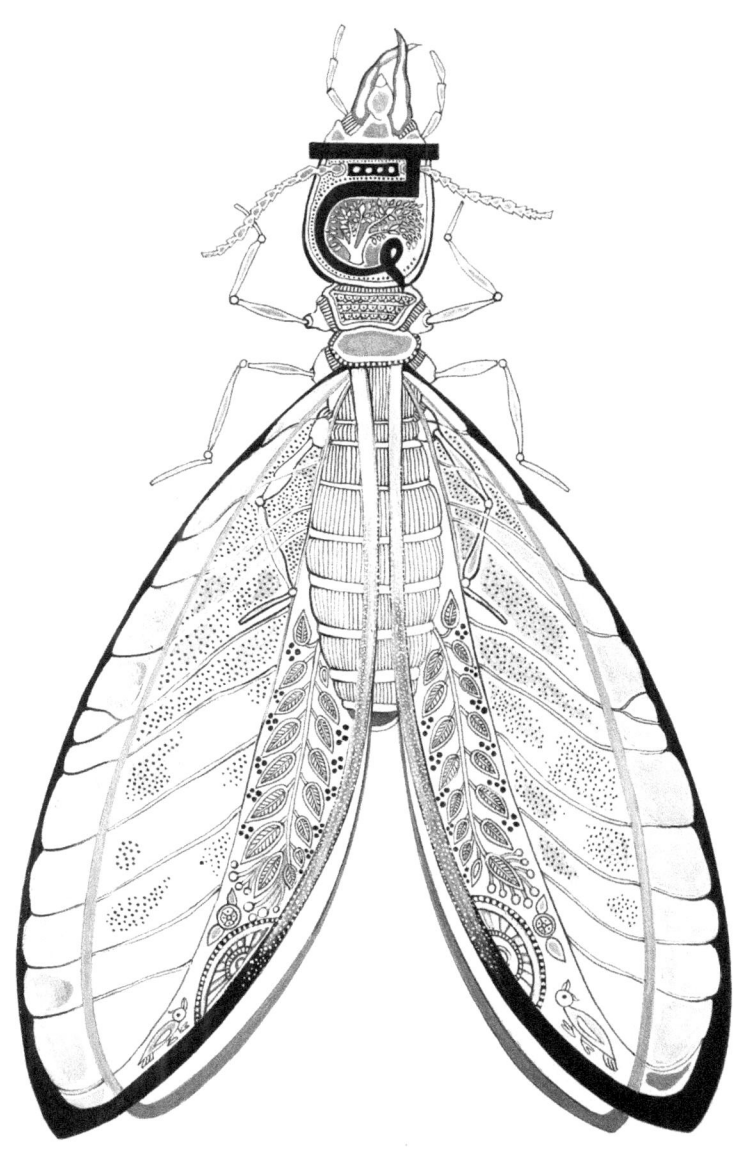

ध

धरती *(dhartī)* – earth

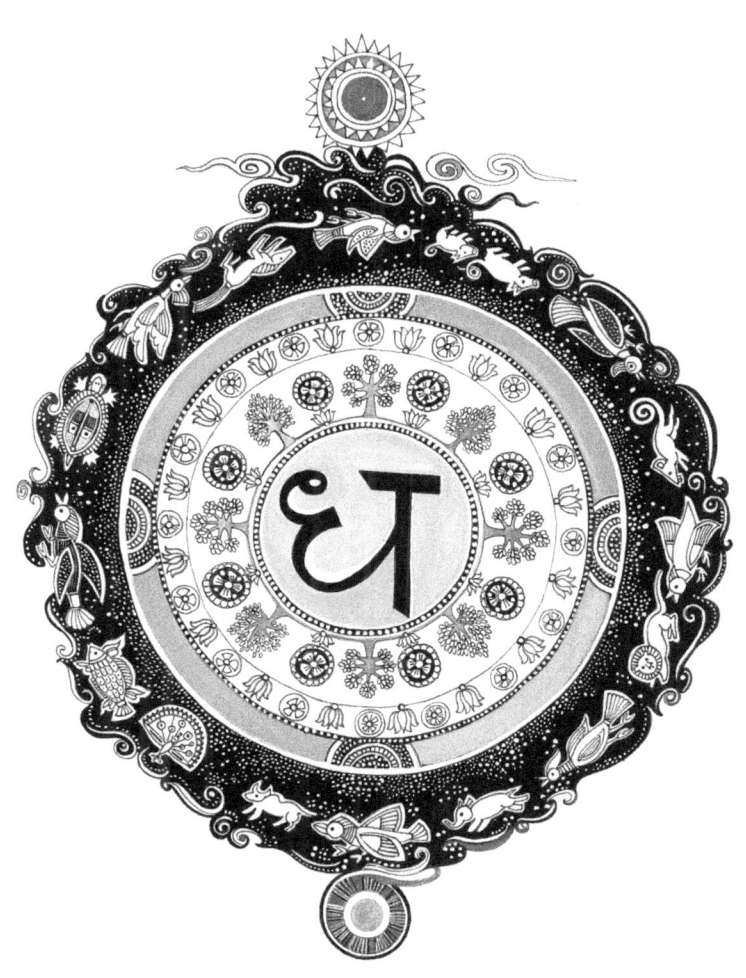

न

न्यग्रोध (*nyagrodh*) – banyan tree

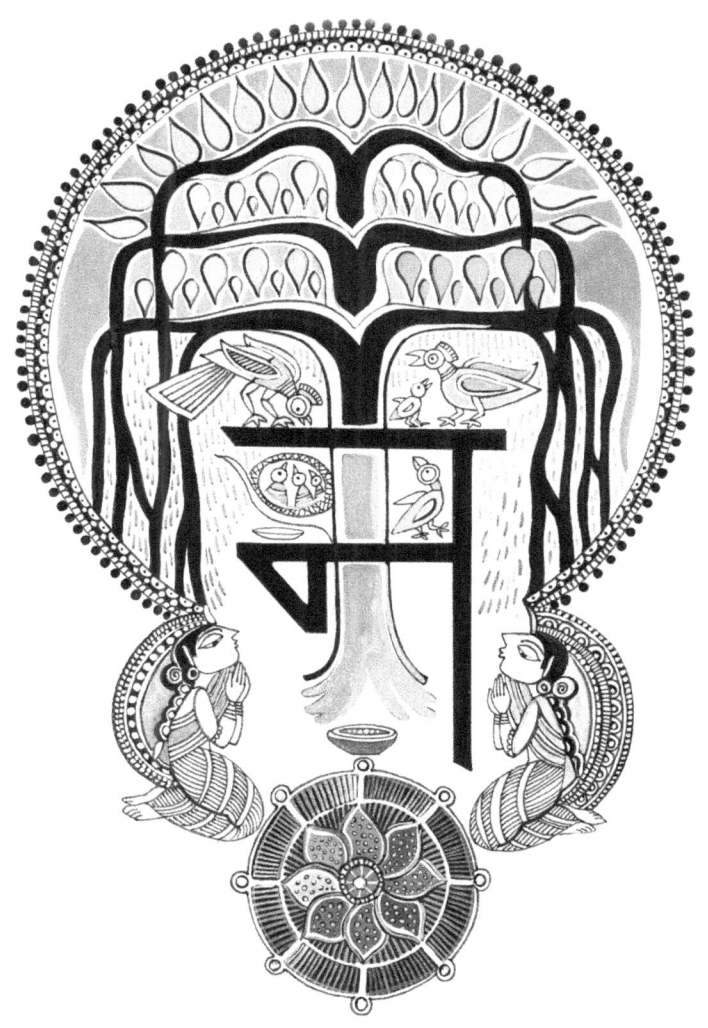

प

पक्षी (*pakshī*) – bird

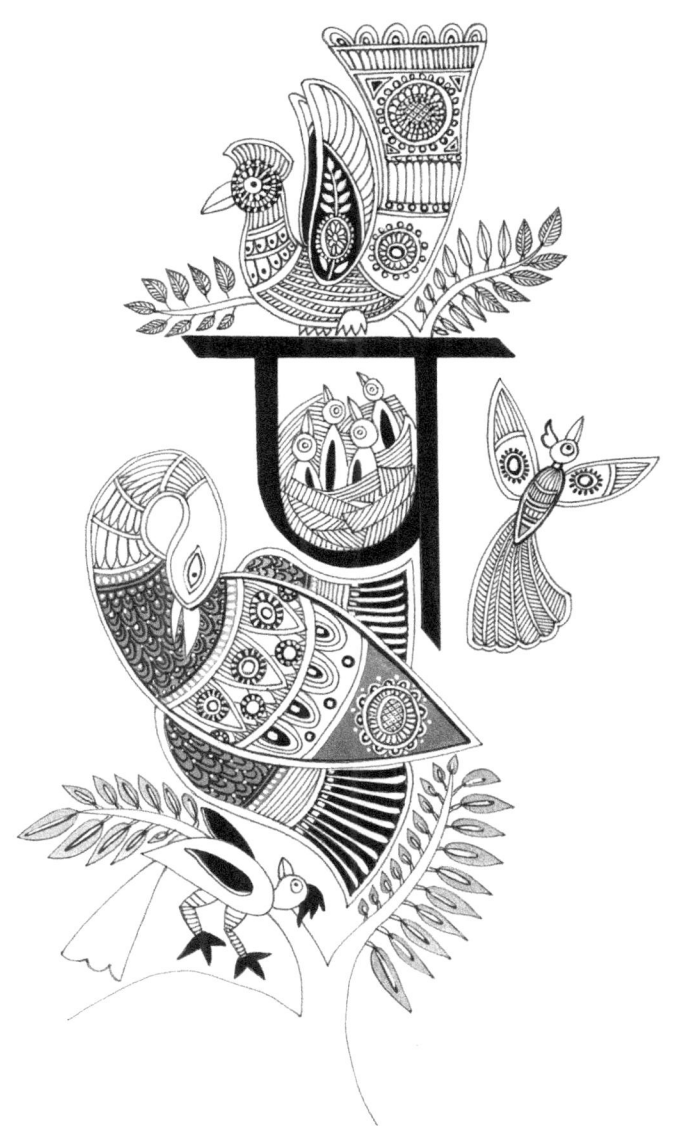

फ

फूल (*phūl*) – flower

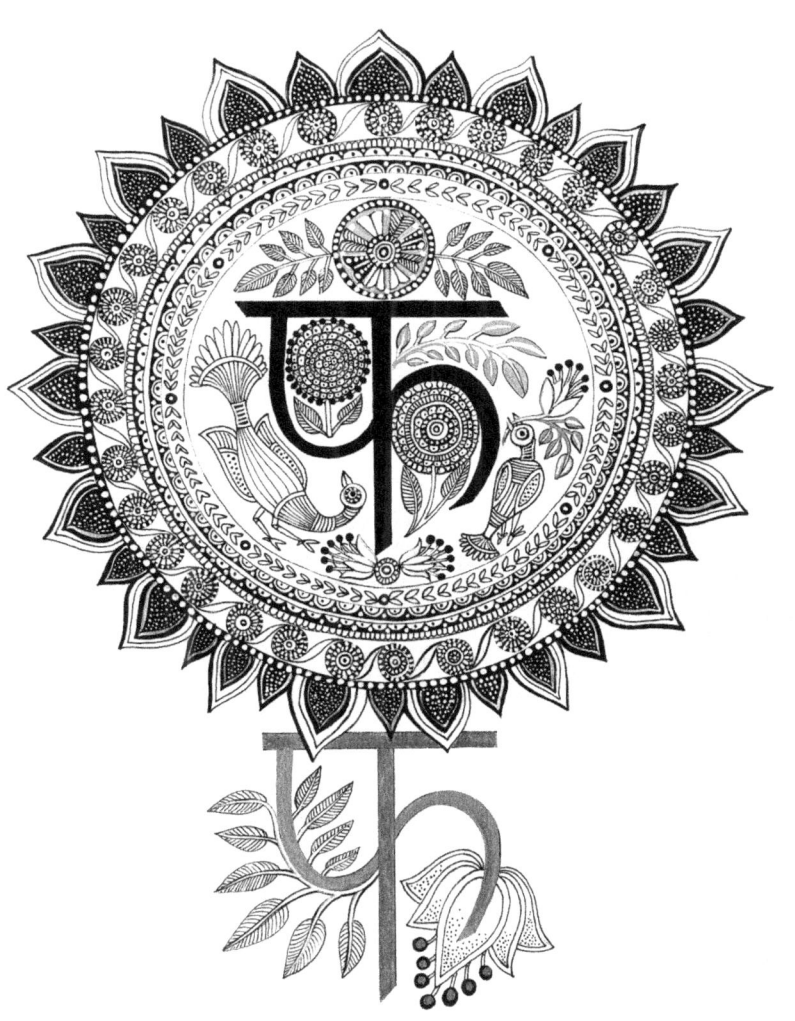

ब

बाज (*bāj*) – hawk

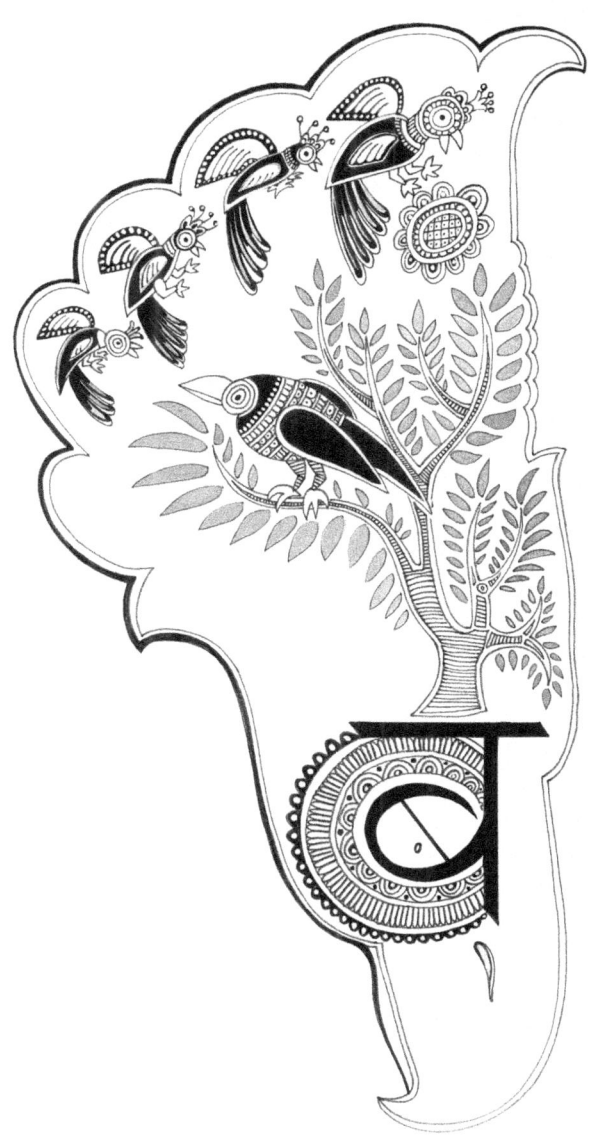

भ

भालू *(bhālū)* – bear

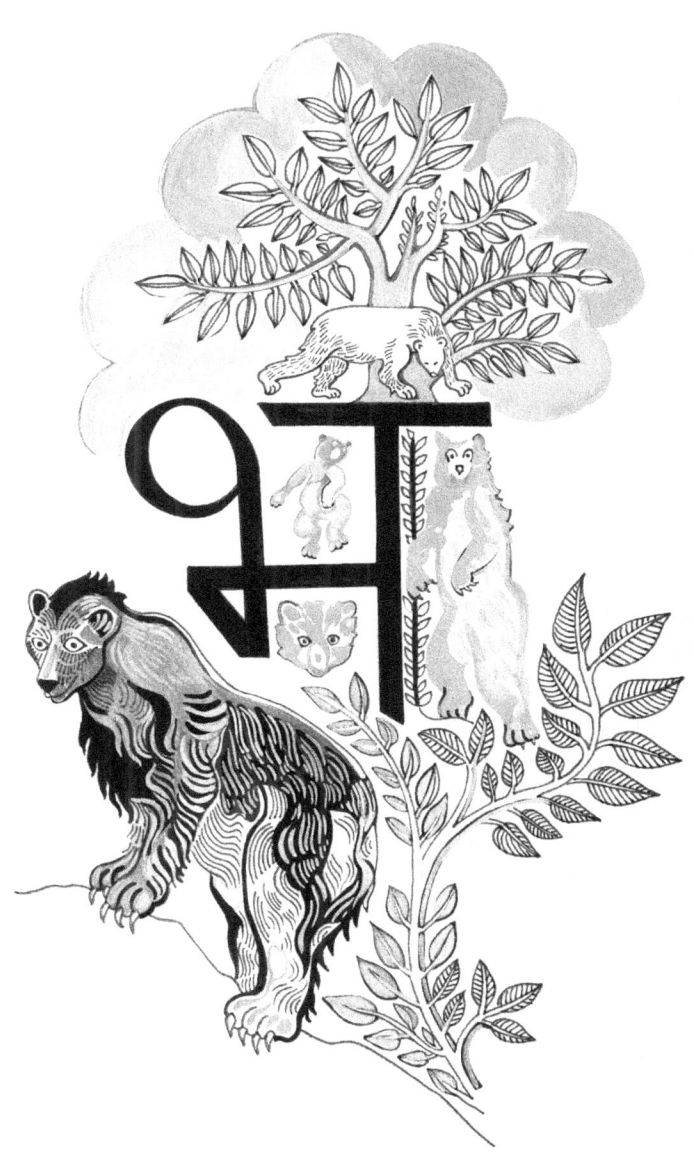

म

मछली (*machalī*) – fish

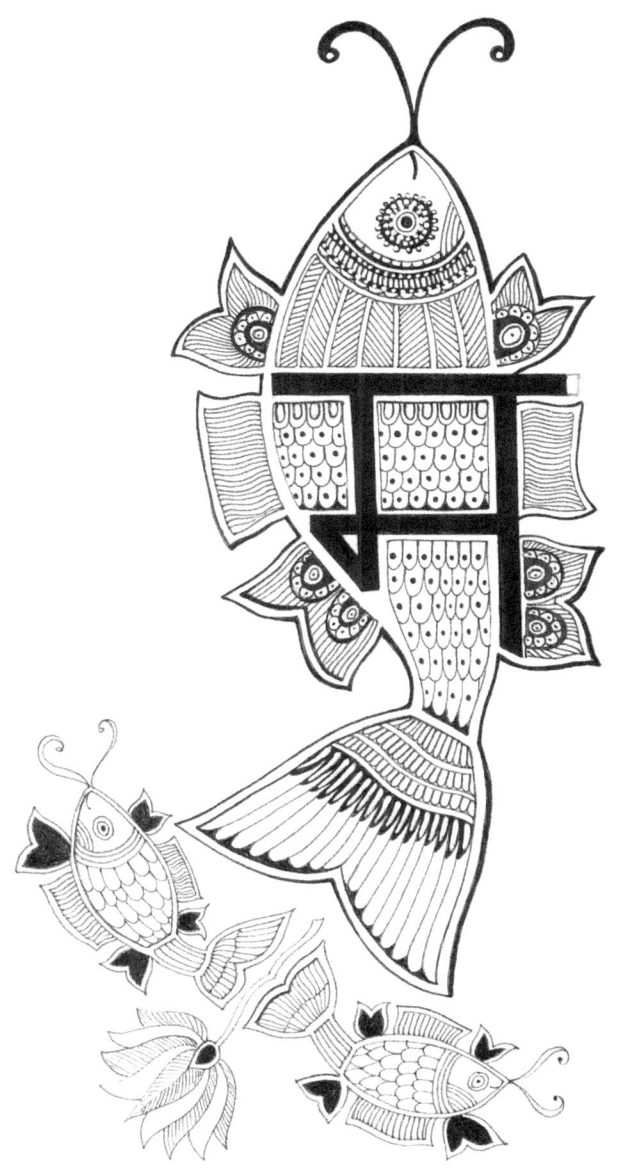

य

युग (*yug*) – period of time, era

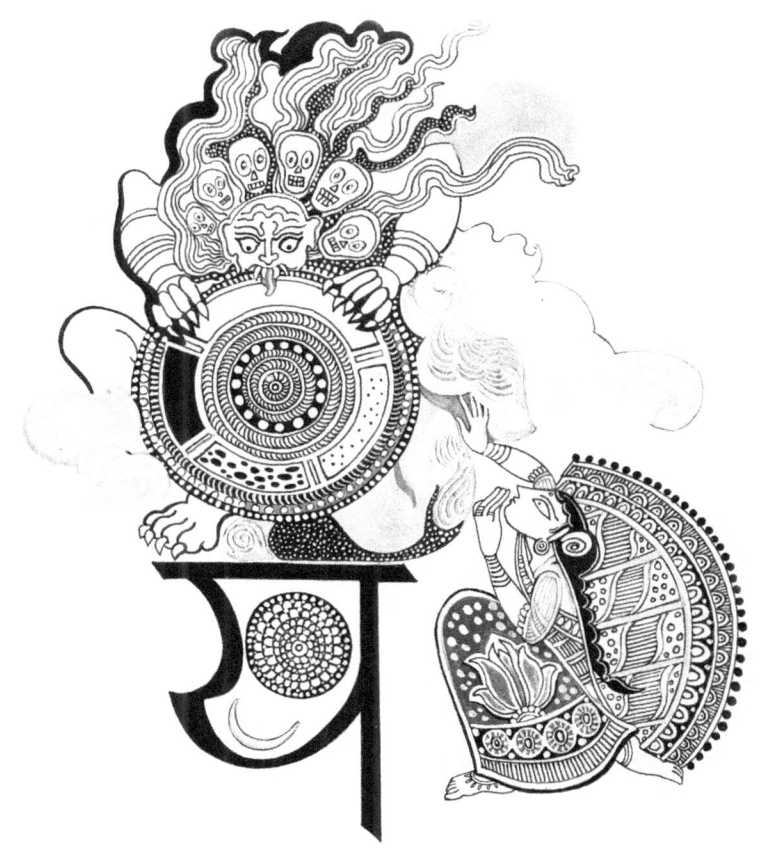

र

रेशम कीड़ा (*resham kīḍā*) – silk worm

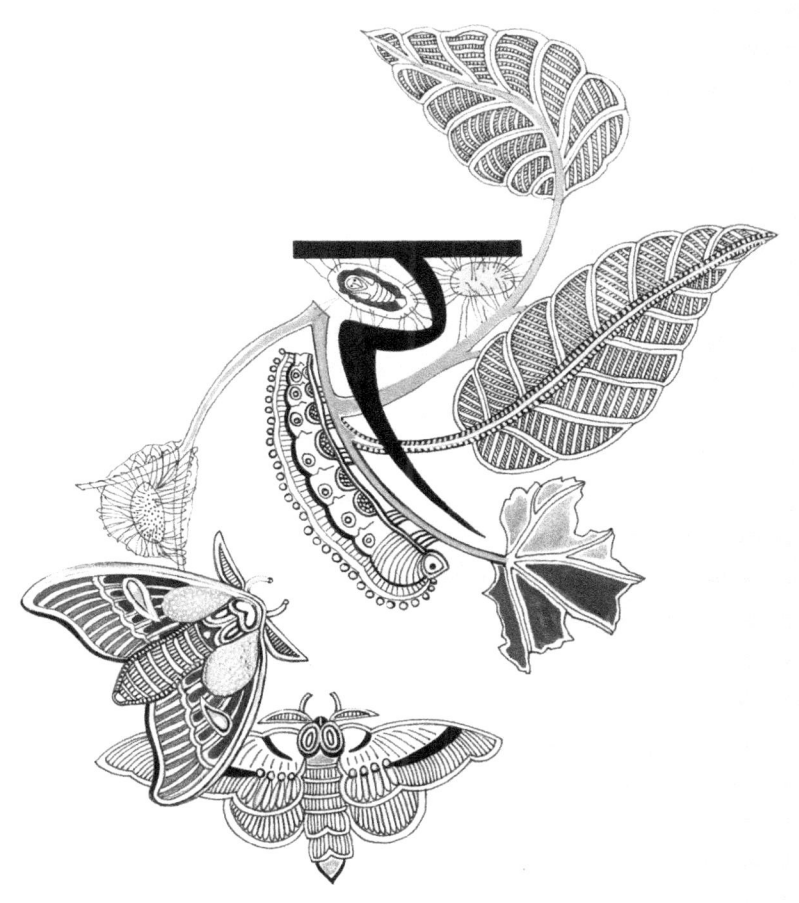

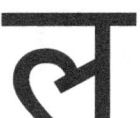

लाइलेक (*lāilek*) – lilac flower

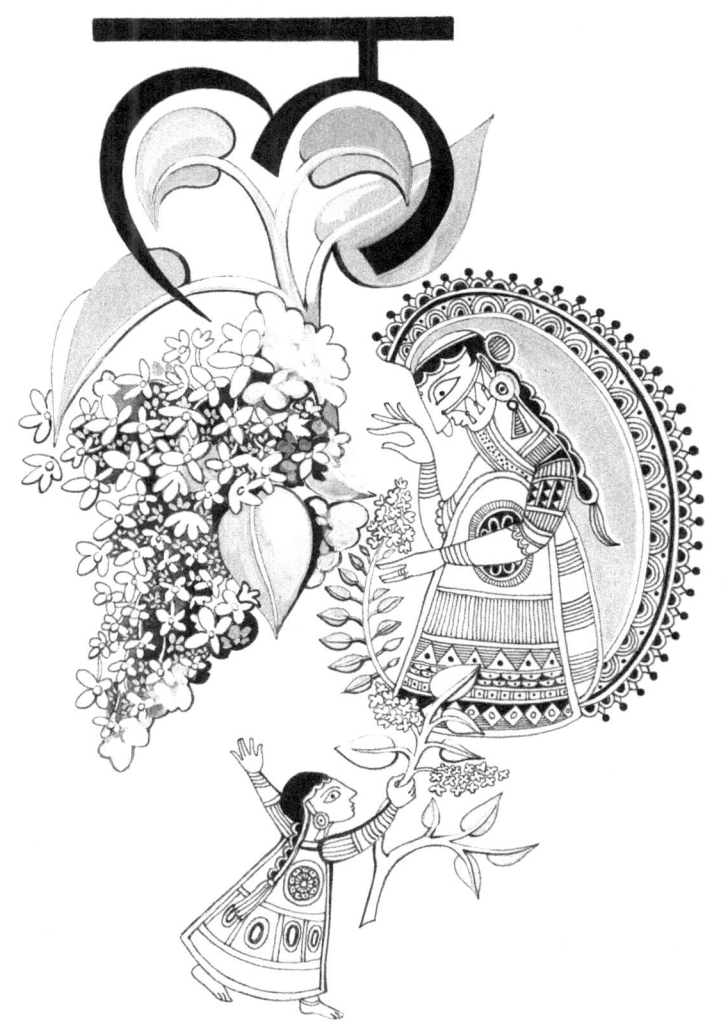

व

वराह (*varāha*) – Varaha

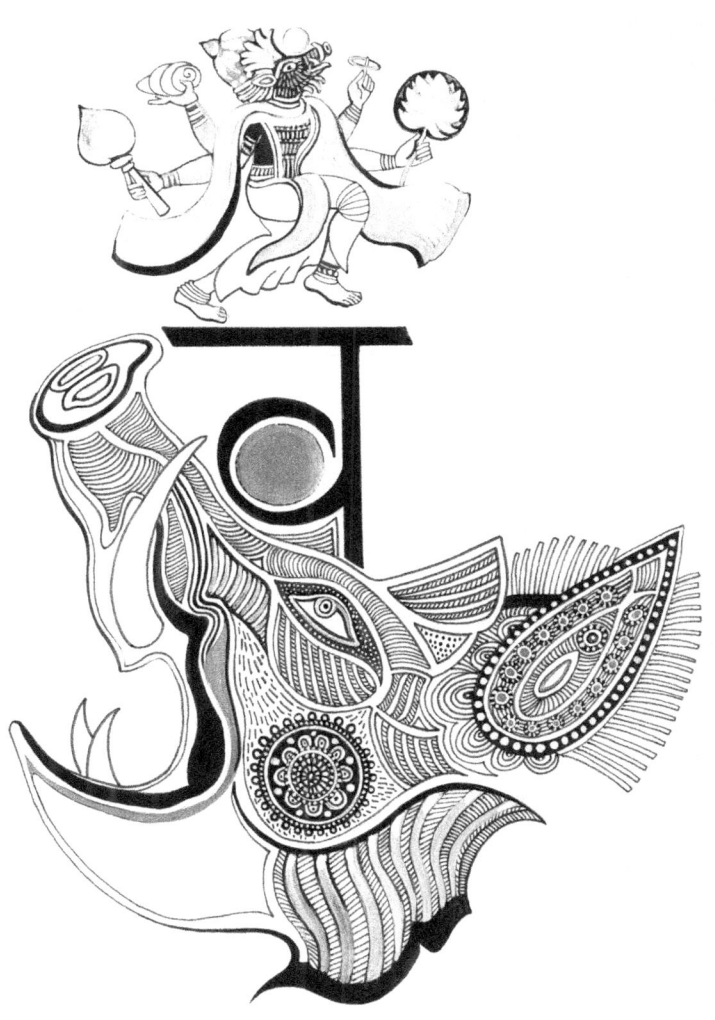

श

शेर (*sher*) – tiger

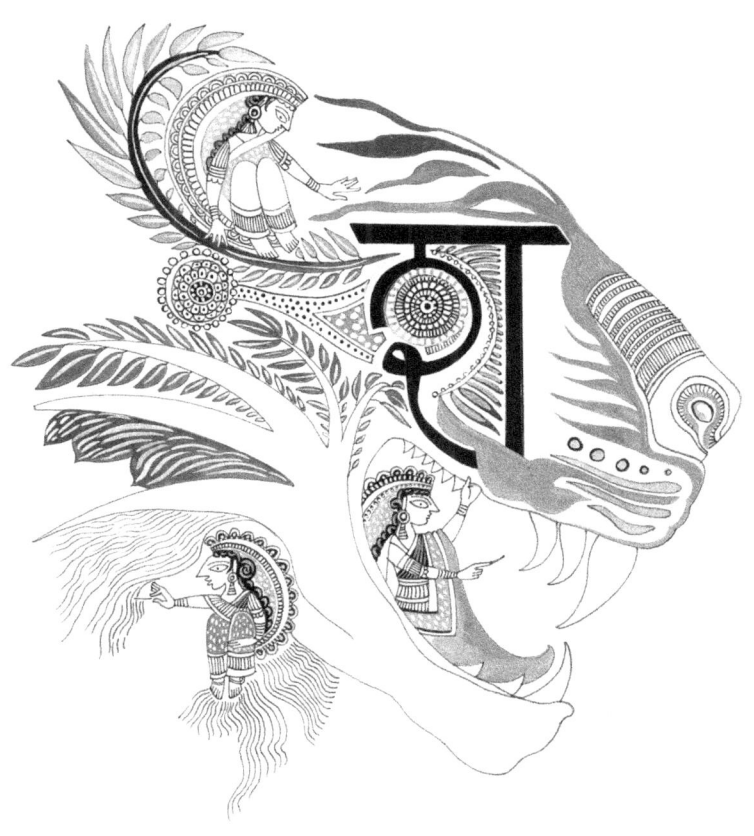

स

सांप (*sānp*) – snake

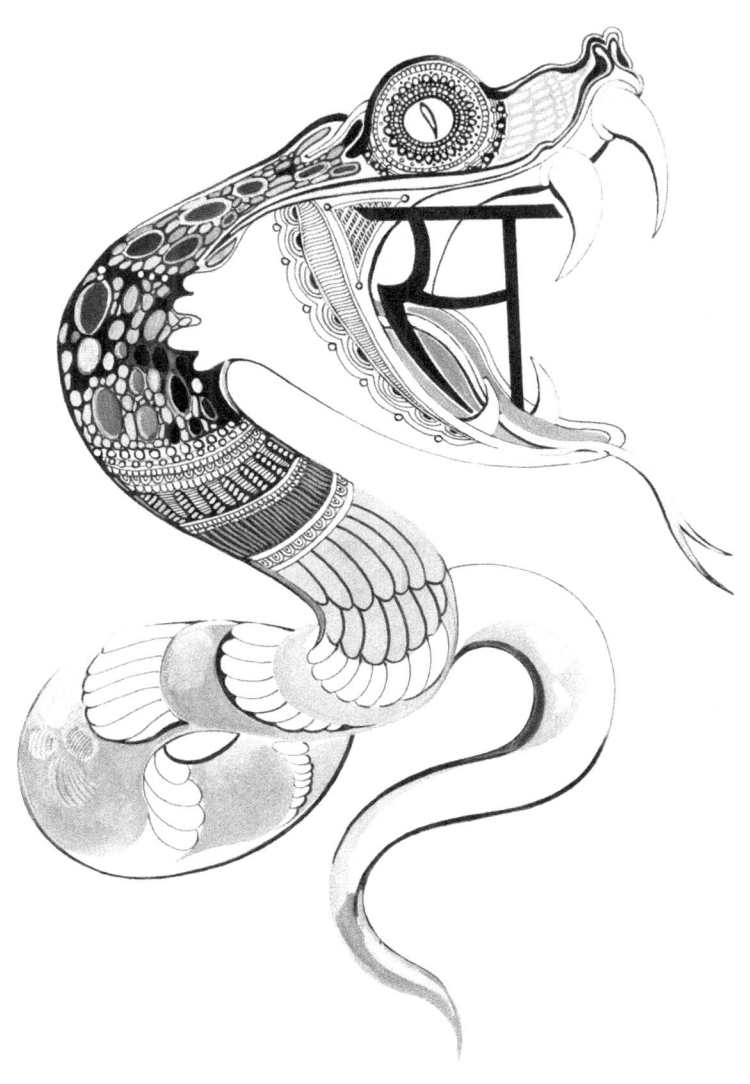

ष

षड्यंत्र (*shadyantra*) – conspiracy

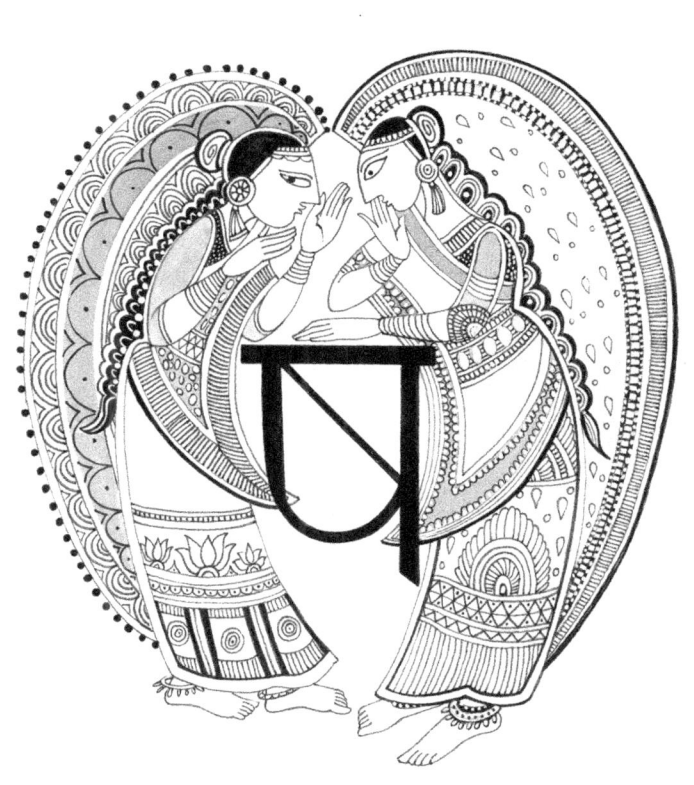

ह

हाथी (*hāthī*) – elephant

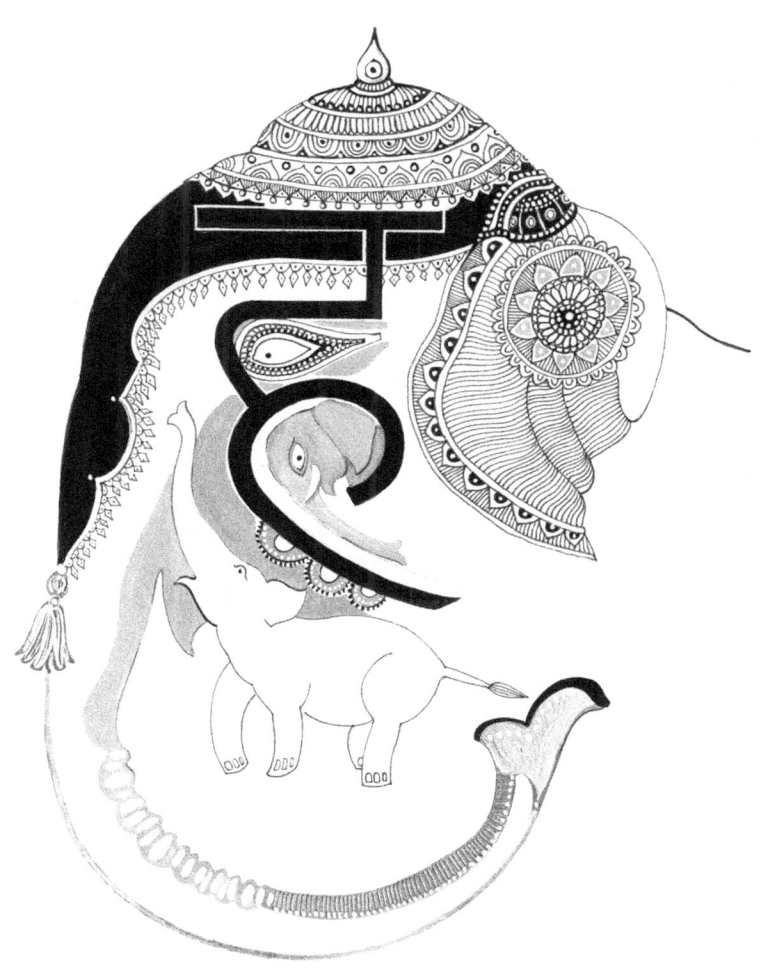

www.ingramcontent.com/pod-product-compliance
Lightning Source LLC
Chambersburg PA
CBHW072228170526
45158CB00002BA/795